RADICAL LOVE

Following the Way of Jesus

ADOLFO QUEZADA

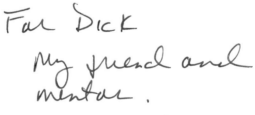

For Dick
My friend and
mentor.

love,
Adolfo

Paulist Press
New York/ Mahwah, NJ

Cover design by Sharyn Banks
Book design by Lynn Else

Library of Congress Cataloging-in-Publication Data

Quezada, Adolfo.
    Radical love : following the way of Jesus / Adolfo Quezada.
        p. cm.
    ISBN 978-0-8091-4637-6 (alk. paper)
    1. God—Love. 2. Jesus Christ—Person and offices. 3. Spiri-
tuality. 4. Love—Religious aspects—Christianity. I. Title.
    BT140.Q49 2010
    231´.6—dc22

                                                      2009018482

Published by Paulist Press
997 Macarthur Boulevard
Mahwah, New Jersey 07430

www.paulistpress.com

Printed and bound in the
United States of America

CONTENTS

Preface   v

Chapter One: The God of Jesus   1

Chapter Two: Radical Love   8

Chapter Three: Rooted in Prayer   15

Chapter Four: God above All   23

Chapter Five: Instinct of the Soul   30

Chapter Six: The Fruit of the Vine   37

Chapter Seven: The Way of the Soul   45

Chapter Eight: Salt of the Earth   50

Chapter Nine: Light of the World   57

Chapter Ten: Sent into the World   64

Chapter Eleven: Blessed Beloved   72

Coda   79

For my sisters Franzia, Maria, and Alicia
In loving remembrance

PREFACE

I was touched by the love of God, and nothing was the same. I entered a place in the soul I had never been before. My love for God intensified beyond description, and my love of self was real and grounded. Love for others became profuse. I could barely contain the charity in my heart. Even the most unlovable were lovable to me, and I no longer had to judge them or convert them or even understand them. I only had to love them.

I felt related to every person. I was compassionate and connected. There grew in me a deep respect for others because I knew we all belonged to the whole. It was as though I had ceased to exist as a separate entity, yet I was fully aware of my individuality. It was a paradox filled with splendor.

All my plans and schemes melted into one purpose: to let God love through me. All else seemed superfluous, petty, and silly. It was not self-annihilation that I sought, nor sameness with the rest. Rather, my soul moved toward reconciliation of opposites, appreciation of diversity, reparation of brokenness, and acceptance of the human and divine interlaced in love.

This was my experience. It was personal, yet by no means unique. The love of God overtakes us when we least expect it. Sometimes our awareness of divine love is gradual; other times it is sudden; always it is profound and transformational. It is not that God suddenly decides to love us. Rather, the love of God is with us always, but it is not until we stop what we are doing and open up our hearts and minds that we can consciously receive the gift and become vessels of divine love.

The soul is the womb of life, the cradle of our being. The love of God is the spirit that ignites our essence and thrusts us into conscious living. Within us are earth and water, for we are soul. Within us are fire and air, for we are spirit. This is the alchemy that affects our lives according to the will of God. Soul awaits the touch of spirit, and this encounter is the genesis of our becoming.

When Jesus was asked by a lawyer to name the most important of God's commandments according to scripture, he answered the lawyer by citing the law. Jesus, a Jew who had studied the law and the prophets, referred to portions of the Torah. "Jesus answered, 'The first is, "Hear O Israel: the Lord our God, the Lord is one; you shall love the Lord your God with all your heart, and with all your soul, and with all your mind, and with all your strength." The second is this, "You shall love your neighbor as yourself." There is no other commandment greater than these'" (Mark 12:29–31). Jesus believed that from this law came all the others. It was the commandment that was in consonance with the purpose of his life: to be the love of God in the world.

This book is called *Radical Love* not because the love of Jesus was extreme, though it was, but because his belief in love was deeply rooted in his own intimate and familiar relationship with God. To be "radical" is to go to the root or origin of something. It is to be thoroughgoing or extreme. "Radical" describes the depth and breadth of the love Jesus had for God and for all creation.

Before anyone had even thought of the term "Christianity" many were already following the teachings of Jesus. They called it following "The Way." Jesus taught about many themes, including faith, mercy, compassion, courage, and forgiveness, but all of these themes and many more were rooted in the one main theme that permeated his ministry and his teachings: that theme was radical love. Thus, the title of this book is *Radical Love: Following the Way of Jesus*.

Although *all* love emanates from divine love, this book focuses on radical love, which comes from the marriage between eros and agape. Eros, which is our impulse to unite and create, moves us naturally toward more excellent being. It is the power that carries us to God and the spirit that animates our soul. Agape is the aspect of divine love that flows through our hearts into the world.

Radical love has no rhyme or reason. It needs no reciprocation or appreciation, and it does not require a certain set of circumstances in order to exist. Conditions may change or fall away, but radical love exists for its own sake.

We follow the way of Jesus by letting go of that which separates us from God, whatever that happens to be. We fall from the wheat stalk of life into the ground of our humanity and become vulnerable to the transformation that comes. As we disintegrate, we receive the nourishment of the soil of love that penetrates our souls. Our lives are rooted in faith and give birth to the fruit of today and the seed of tomorrow.

CHAPTER ONE

THE GOD OF JESUS

Yoked with the Divine

The invitation to be yoked with God is a proposal of spiritual marriage. To accept it is to enter into an intimate union in which the "I" and the "Thou" fall away and only the "I Am" is left.

Jesus echoed the invitation of God: "Come to me, all you that are weary and are carrying heavy burdens, and I will give you rest. Take my yoke upon you, and learn from me; for I am gentle and humble in heart; and you will find rest for your souls. For my yoke is easy, and my burden is light" (Matt 11:28).

This is an invitation to be yoked with the divine in all aspects of our lives. In radical love we come to God not so that our labor or the burden we carry may be lifted from us, but so that we can confront life as one *with* God. The rest that we are offered is repose of the soul. Yoked with the divine, we receive the energy of radical love with which to live our lives. From God we learn simplicity, humility, and gentleness.

Radical love surrenders all and seeks nothing for itself, but it is grateful for all that comes its way. To love radically is to live abundantly and to die impoverished. Radical love gives until there is no more to give, and then it gives away its poverty. We do not measure out the love that we offer to others because love is infinite and cannot be depleted. Radical love is passionate and involves us wholeheartedly, yet because radical love emanates from God, it is never out of control or fanatical in nature. Radical love begets passion, not the other way around.

The radical love we have for one another is but a reflection of God's radical love for us. Our foundational reality of being is radical love, and from this essence all else derives. Radical love is the energy of God that creates and animates all that is. Dante believed that "love moves the Sun and the stars," but radical love also opens our minds to wider horizons and deeper truths, and it opens our hearts to forgiveness of others and forgetfulness of self.

The Centrality of God

The life of Jesus was based on the centrality of God. He loved others as he was loved by God. But the purity in Jesus' heart had less to do with his goodness than with his nondualistic approach to life. For Jesus there was only God, and everything else followed from that. What mattered most to him was that his thoughts, emotions, and actions be congruent with the will of God.

The God of Jesus was not a mental construct, a conceptual structure, or a set of religious beliefs. Jesus had studied the Jewish scriptures, but he knew God personally because he was in God and God was in him. For Jesus, God was his actual experience of life. He looked at the world through the eyes of God and from this divine perspective, there was no isolation, no separation—all was one.

Jesus taught that every person's relationship with God is an intensely personal and private affair. He did not question the need for organization in religion, but he protested vehemently when the organization interfered with a person's access to God. He revered God, yet he enjoyed a special familiarity with God. The God whom Jesus called "Abba" (daddy, papa, or dada) was nearer to him than he was to himself.

Jesus believed that the personal relationship between us and God affects our relationship with all of creation. Because he loved God radically, he loved the children who gathered around him. He loved the sparrows, the lilies, and the mountains. Jesus loved his family and his friends and those whom he called his disciples. He taught that one could not truly love and serve God without also loving and serving all human beings. For him, to love one is to love the other because essentially they are one.

Jesus imagined a conversation between God and those persons who had loved and served others during their lifetimes. God said, "I was hungry and you gave me food, I was thirsty and you gave me something to drink, I was a stranger and you welcomed me, I was naked and you gave me clothing, I was sick and you took care of me, I was in prison and you visited me" (Matt 25:35–36).

Those persons who had loved and served their fellow-human beings were puzzled at God's words. They remembered reaching out to others, but not necessarily to God. Then, according to Jesus, God assured them, "[J]ust as you did it to one of the least of these who are members of my family, you did it to me" (Matt 25:40).

Precious in the Eyes of God

The God of Jesus loves each person and each creature of the universe with the radical love of a mother. "Can a woman forget her nursing child, or show no compassion for the child of her womb? Even these may forget, yet I will not forget you" (Isa 49:15). As a mother caresses her newborn baby and gently touches every inch of its body to make sure it is all right, so does God cherish every living being and knows intimately its nature and condition. "Are not five sparrows sold for two pennies?" Jesus asked. "Yet not one of them is forgotten in God's sight. But even the hairs on your head are all counted" (Luke 12:6–7).

Some believe that the purpose of love is to form a whole that is greater than the sum of its parts. Jesus believed that the purpose of love is to cherish each part as if it were the whole unto itself. He asked, "If a shepherd has a hundred sheep, and one of them has gone astray, does he not leave the ninety-nine on the mountains and go in search of the one that went astray? And if he finds it, truly I tell you, he rejoices over it more than over the ninety-nine that never went astray" (Matt 18:12–13). We are each precious in the eyes of God.

The radical love of Jesus was all-inclusive. Like God, who, Jesus believed, "makes his sun rise on the evil and on the good, and sends rain on the righteous and on the unrighteous" (Matt 5:45), Jesus loved indiscriminately. "You have heard that it was said, 'You shall love your neighbor and hate your enemy.' But I say to you, Love your enemies and pray for those who persecute you" (Matt 5:43–44). This is the nature of radical love, to break through the walls that separate us from one another and therefore from God.

Jesus acknowledged the divine reality within himself, and he recognized it in every person he encountered. To him, every human being was sacred. Nothing mattered more in life to him than the human soul and its marriage to the spirit of God.

At One with God

Jesus did not ask to be worshipped or idolized, only to be loved and followed. He called his disciples to a greater love than they had ever known. He referred to them as the "salt of the earth" and "the light of the world," and he believed in them even when they did not believe in themselves. But he warned them that they could lose their savor and end up in the dark if they did not remain grounded in God. He cared for them and sought their welfare. He allowed them to enter his personal life and shared with them the joy and the grief of his life. "You are my friends" he told them (John 15:14).

When Jesus said to his disciples that he had come so that they "may have life, and have it abundantly" (John 10:10), he did not mean that they could have all that they wanted, but that they could have a life filled with the abundance of God's radical love. When he asked his disciples to deny themselves and follow him, he was not asking them to practice renunciation of their desires, but to love God above all else. All desire pales in contrast to being one with God. This is our magnificent obsession. Jesus believed that "where your treasure is, there your heart will be also" (Matt 6:21).

The radical love of Jesus was paradoxical. It was powerful because it was based on powerlessness. He called on his disciples to lose their lives in order to save their lives, and to receive by giving. The radical love of Jesus challenged his disciples to bless the unjust, love the unlovely, and pray for those who harmed them. Jesus' radical love compelled him to sacrifice even unto death so that God would live through him forever.

For Jesus, service to others was the spontaneous action prompted by a contemplative heart. He did not value prayer over service anymore than he valued service over prayer. When he said to his friend Martha that her sister Mary had chosen "the better part" by tending first to matters of the soul, he was in no way rebuking Martha for her more active approach. Rather, Jesus was telling her that service comes of love and love is the fruit of contemplation. Radical love is the principle of action, and if we want to serve, we must first be willing to receive the radical love of God in our heart through prayer and contemplation.

Keep yourselves in the love of God.
Jude 21

CHAPTER TWO

RADICAL LOVE

Holy Adoration — Prayer

God summons us to the divine milieu and invites us to enter into the intimacy of love. How does the infinite love the finite? It loves totally, completely, perfectly, extravagantly, and radically. God gives us the world, literally, and the cosmos, and life itself. Our attempt to describe the radical love of God, or to measure it by our limited human standards, falls short by far. But we don't have to understand God to love and be loved; we only have to open ourselves to receive this holy adoration.

To be cherished beyond measure, to be unconditionally and totally accepted without shame or prejudice, criticism or judgment—what a freeing reality to experience. This is how God loves us. The radical love of God is not contingent on anything at all. It is ours regardless of who we are or how we live our lives. There is nothing we have to do to earn it or deserve it; we have only to *accept* it.

God loves us with an everlasting love that nurtures our souls and grounds our being. God's radical love encourages us to move out of our comfortable place and enter on the way of the cross that leads to compassionate action on behalf of those who are suffering. God's radical love challenges us to reach for superior heights and venture into greater depths.

The radical love of God is universal, yet God loves us individually. Divine love does not offer itself wholesale, but intimately and personally. It is not humanity that is loved by God, but each human soul that is a part of the whole. It is not creation that is held in the heart of God, but each rock, each tree, each hummingbird, each blade of grass.

The radical love of God is not passive. It pursues us to the ends of the earth and searches for us until we are found. The beauty that our eyes behold in the world and in the heavens is a gift from our Beloved. God courts us with the fragrance of a rose and the sound of ocean waves. God woos us with the sweet taste of fruit and the touch of a baby's skin. In the morning light we hear the voice of God, "Come, my beloved, let us go forth into the fields, and lodge in the villages; let us go out early to the vineyards....There I will give you my love" (Song 7:11–12).

Awakened Intimacy

In the quiet and the still, we know the purpose of our life: to be at one with God, absorbed in radical love of God, and sustained by God's holy presence. Inherent in our humanity is a deep yearning to be with God and to be enveloped in God's unconditional, radical love for us. To seek God with our whole being is the instinct of our soul.

We are overcome with joy when we become aware that we are rooted in God. The joy comes in the dissolution of the self into the absolute. There is a clarity that comes with joy, a clarity about who we are and who we are *not*. We are not that illusion of a fragmentary self with which we identify. We are of the essence of God. We are the manifestation of God in the world. In the realm of love we no longer differentiate ourselves from God. We are not God, but we are *in* God and God is *in* us. In the depths of our prayer we can no longer tell if we are praying to God or if God is praying to us. In truth, we are praying as one.

In radical love, we die to self and resurrect in union with our Beloved. In radical love, we abandon our hold on our separate self and receive the essence of the One to whom we surrender. Losing and gaining, giving and receiving—this is the rhythm of love.

When we love God radically, we enter into an awakened intimacy that dispels the illusion of duality between lover and Beloved. As a result of this wholehearted love for God, we see God in everyone and everything. We see God in the valley of despair and the peak of ecstasy, in the profane and the sacred. There is no place or instance in which we do not experience God.

In God-consciousness we do not transcend our humanness; rather, we allow ourselves to enter fully into it. God-consciousness grounds us in the reality of the world in which we live. No longer is our face lifted toward the heavens in search of the divine. Now we face the person before us; we behold the hummingbird amid the flowers; and we are acutely aware of all that is because it holds the reality of God.

Two Paths

In radical love we give ourselves over completely to God. We live in total abandon, holding nothing back, allowing nothing to keep us from this union.

Our union with God, however, is not unlike a romantic relationship between lovers. In the beginning there is the excitement of being connected with each other. There is pleasure and comfort; there is the joy of special companionship; and there is the yearning for each other's presence. There is ecstasy beyond measure as boundaries drop away and identities are blurred.

There are two paths that a love relationship can take. On the first, lovers are lost in each other and don't really *want* to be found. It is a private affair, a one-on-one proposition. If others enter their circle of bliss, they are considered interlopers. If one lover or the other looks away or is distracted by anything or anyone, jealousy ensues. Fear of losing this paradisiacal state gives rise to possessiveness. Then it is just a matter of time before this love affair deteriorates into a hate affair, leaving disillusionment and lamentation in its wake.

The second path for lovers leads to a deeper, everlasting relationship. Rather than isolating themselves and hoarding their love for their exclusive benefit, they allow the love to touch others outside of their private circle. Their love is still blissful, yet they are not inebriated or blinded by its intensity. In sharing their love with others, it grows and is life-giving. Because their love is not insecure, it does not become jealous or possessive. Unlike a flower that is kept under glass, their love flourishes and offers its beauty to the world. The yearning for each other's presence is still there, but it is filled with great anticipation rather than desperation.

The first path is focused on intense feelings and on what one can get out of the relationship. The second path is focused on self-giving. The first leads to enmeshment; the second to union. The first squelches individuality; the second encourages it. The first depends on fervency to stay alive; the second is grounded in authenticity and trust. The first is an ephemeral relationship; the second is an eternal marriage.

Ultimate Surrender

Divine love is always present, although sometimes we don't recognize it. It is with us regardless of circumstances and despite our behavior. But only when we stop long enough to catch our breath do we begin to experience the transformation that comes with such ever-present love.

The radical love between ourselves and God is consummated, that is, made perfect, when we consent to bring the seed of divine life to fruition in the world. We say to God, "For your love is better than wine, your anointing oils are fragrant, your name is poured out;…Draw me after you." God says to us, "Arise, my love, my fair one, and come away" (Song 1.2–4, 2:10). Into the dark chambers of our souls, God infuses love, and light enters darkness.

Conscious of our oneness with God, we want nothing else. Having the wisdom that is born of love, we do not crave knowledge. Having the willingness to sacrifice everything, even our life, for the sake of love, we neither seek nor fear power.

The paradox we face in loving God is that God is the ultimate source of the love we hold for God. Because our love for God is rooted in divine love, it is radical love, and radical love is, above all, radical surrender. But surrender does not mean annihilation. Instead, we release our illusions of power, perfection, privilege, and control. We give up our narcissism and egocentricity. We lose our concern about what is going to happen to us and what is going to satisfy us.

In this ultimate surrender, we move beyond our self, toward union with God. We open ourselves to the power of love and the hope of possibility. We yield to divine intelligence and listen to the wisdom that emanates from the depths of our soul.

Through prayer and contemplation we acknowledge our integrality with God. The veil of our individuality drops away, and we let go of our illusion of separation. Our breath becomes the breath of God; our thoughts yield to the mind of God; our emotions move through ecstasy and beyond, into a peace beyond description. Our love intensifies until it burns away all that is not real. Now only God is left. No longer do we love—now we are love.

...as you are being rooted and grounded in love.
Ephesians 3:17

CHAPTER THREE

ROOTED IN PRAYER

Returning

We pray because it is in our human nature to reconnect with our Creator. It is a stronger instinct than that of a newborn clinging to its mother. It is more like a river returning to the ocean. We long to be with God because in God's holy presence we are most truly ourselves.

In prayer we are naked and unmasked. Here is where we face the truth, and the truth does set us free. Here is where we dare to be authentic, since with God we can be no less. Prayer is a coming home, a returning to the heart of God.

Only through the intimate act of prayer can we reconnect with God. Through prayer our hardened hearts melt, and the barriers fall away. Through prayer we become open and allow ourselves to receive the redeeming, radical love of God.

My heart longs for a sacred space, a place of rest, a place of peace. It matters not if it is simple or ornate, as long as I can enter there and pray.

Oh, holy ground, you welcome me, you call forth all believers. My hungry soul and thirsty mind are nourished and refreshed. Here is where I want to be, where spirit leads, and love abides.

We are drawn to the still and silent hour of contemplation. It is here in this time and space of divine influence that we come to know our purpose and to discover the meaning of our existence.

In this hour of contemplation we commend our life to God. We may carry with us a sense of outrage over wrongs that have been done to us or to others, but in the light of contemplation the shadows disappear and we are granted the power to forgive.

We may come burdened with the heavy load of guilt, but in the absolution of contemplation we meet our humble self and embrace all of who we are: the good and the bad. It is from this state of humility that the tension of pride and possession is released, and our path is redirected.

We may come to this sacred hour with broken hearts and shattered dreams, but in the restoration of contemplation we are made whole, if only for another day. In the hour of contemplation the noise dies down and our hardness is dissolved. Our minds begin to see, and our hearts begin to listen.

When we pray, we enter womb space. Here we rest from the rigors of life. Here we restore our spirit and re-create our soul. No words or thoughts are necessary, no rituals or incantations; we need only the belief that we belong with God, whose radical love induces our return.

Responding

In prayer it is we who are responding to God's will and not the other way around. It is not a matter of deciding what we need in life and then begging or cajoling God to meet these needs. God created us and knows us better than we know ourselves. God is our source and our sustenance. As a mother gives birth to a child and then cares for it with unconditional love, so does God fulfill our needs even before we know what they are.

When we ask anything from God, other than God, we are using God rather than allowing God to use us. Jesus asks that we seek the realm of God within us, and everything we truly need will be given to us.

When we pray to God for direction or guidance in our decision making, God does not respond by telling us what to do. God does not give answers or point out the best road for us to take. Rather, when we pray, we make ourselves available to the God within us, who is infinite intelligence, wisdom, and understanding. In prayer, we tap those resources within that help us make the best decision possible.

> *You are the spirit that animates my being, the love that flows through my veins. I stop and listen to the sound of your breath and the beating of your heart. You are life and you are death, the alpha and the omega. You are all, and I am in you.*

Our prayer is more than a petition for what we want or need. It is a declaration to God of our love. It is a love song from the depths of our soul. In prayer we surrender our illusion of control. In prayer we yearn for God alone and seek for God with no purpose but to enter into God's holy presence.

When, through prayer, we enter our innermost self, we become aware that there is no separation between lover and Beloved. In prayer, we remember who we are. We remember God in every moment, with every breath.

We live out our daily lives in what we consider ordinary ways, but as we do, we are absorbed in God. Our thoughts, our actions, our very existence is pervaded with our magnificent obsession with God. Nothing in life or death is more important to us than being with God.

Attending

How exhilarating it is to become immersed in a campaign for justice. How rewarding to gather food to feed many who would not otherwise be nourished. How good it feels to be available to our friends as they confront life's difficulties. Yet, these feelings of exhilaration, accomplishment, and goodness are not enough to keep us responding day after day as life requires. Only the frequent return to the fountain of prayer can refresh us sufficiently to be about the business of radical love.

Before we can attend to the needs of the world we must first attend to our own most basic need: to receive the divine energy that only prayer can give us. Because we are needed on the front lines of the crusade for justice, and the abolishment of disease and poverty, we must first prepare ourselves in prayer. In prayer, we gather our resources and receive our marching orders. In the clarity of prayer we can distinguish between our will and God's. In prayer, we are emboldened to charge ahead in the face of adversity and conflict.

Beloved Being, Life of my life, avail yourself of me. Your will becomes my will. I am your sight, your voice, your touch. I am your presence and your love. Send me to the suffering, send me to the dying. Send me to the poor and lost.

In our quest for inspiration we must first build the nest in which inspiration can be born. The discipline of prayer, in whatever place and in whatever fashion, is the nest that we prepare. We can do the work of heaven, but only when we stop long enough to gather before we sow, to learn before we teach, and to rest before we create.

Prayer, that is, remembering God as our source and destiny, is as much a regular part of our daily life as eating, sleeping, or even breathing. We create habits and routines that assist us to remember the most important thing we do—attend to God. The more we are absorbed in God, the more we are sent out into the highways and byways to do God's bidding. But always, we return in prayer to our Beloved.

Persevering — in spir'lardity

Sometimes our inability to pray may be a sign that we have unfinished business to which we must attend. "So when you are offering your gift at the altar, if you remember that your brother or sister has something against you, leave your gift there before the altar and go; first be reconciled to your brother or sister, and then come and offer your gift" (Matt 5:23–24).

God is always available to us, no matter what. But we cannot be fully open to God if our heart is full of rancor toward another who is part of God. It is essential that we make peace with our brothers and sisters even as we make peace with God.

Sometimes, however, our inability to pray has no explanation, and we feel powerless in our attempt to reconnect with God. There are times in our lives when we simply cannot pray. No matter how hard we try or how much faith we muster, we do not feel connected to God. During these times of spiritual aridity, the more we try to get close to God, the farther away God seems. We can listen to one hundred sermons, read many spiritual books, attend church regularly, and do good deeds, and still feel spiritually disconnected.

Then we remember that our faith is not in our feelings of connectedness or the peace in our hearts, but rather in the constancy of God, regardless of what we may be feeling at the time. Faith is not contingent on what we experience emotionally, but on our belief that, no matter what, God is with us.

docta ignorantia

> *You, who have no name, are known to my heart.*
> *You, who have no face, are seen by my soul.*
> *You, who are silent, are heard in my silence.*
> *You, who are elusive, are with me evermore.*

When the gift of prayer seems lost to us, we pray anyway. If we want to pray and cannot do it, then perseverance is our prayer. If we want to pray and our heart is silent, then silence is our prayer. If we want to pray and God seems absent, then faith is our prayer. When we can't pray as we want, we pray as we can.

Then when you call upon me and come and pray to me, I will hear you. When you search for me, you will find me; if you seek me with all your heart, I will let you find me, says the Lord.
Jeremiah 29:12–14

CHAPTER FOUR

GOD ABOVE ALL

Holding Nothing Back

To love God with all our heart means that we love God above all else. Even the love we have for others and for creation is but an emanation of the love between ourselves and God. Our wholehearted love for God manifests itself in our daily life by the choices we make. In every instance, no matter the occasion, we choose to be with God over any other possibility. To love God with all our heart means that we recognize the divine in everyone and everything. We experience God living in us with every beat of our heart.

To love God with all our mind does not mean that we are always thinking about God. It means that we are always God-conscious. This means that God is the source of our every thought. Distractions come and we are carried away, yet our love for God compels us to make the return to God-consciousness. This radical love between ourselves and God compels us to live fully and abundantly in the present moment. We are mindful of God's ubiquity wherever we may be.

To love God with all our soul means that we surrender our very being to God. We can't capture God in our heart, and we can't understand God in our mind, but we *can* be with God in our soul. To love God with all our soul means that we return to the depths of our soul regularly and frequently in prayer and contemplation and attend to God. We attend to God, not because God needs our attention, but because attention is an integral part of love. Radical love prompts us to tend and attend to our Beloved.

We love God with all our strength when we walk in humility in the light of God, and when we live according to the truth as we know it. We love God with all our strength when we trust in love, and when we confront whatever comes with a courageous heart.

To love God with all our heart, with all our soul, with all our mind and strength means that we love God with our whole being, holding nothing back. It means that we dedicate our life to becoming the means through which God can love the world. It means that we carry God within us everywhere we go, even into the darkest and deepest abyss. To love God in this way requires that we walk with God, talk with God, be with God, live with God, and die with God.

Even in the Darkness

One moment we are living the love of God and basking in the intimacy of union, and suddenly it is as if we have been expelled from Paradise! The sense of God's presence eludes us, and we feel alone and lost. Where once there was a garden full and fresh, there now is left the remnant of a sacred time. God's immanence was clear, and it filled our heart and brought us to a higher place, but now it's gone. Silent is God's voice; absent is God's love—or so it seems.

As we mourn our loss and pine for what has been, we can barely love at all. But it is in this loveless place that we discover faith. Gone are the lofty feelings that buoyed us in rough waters. Absent are the signs that assured us all was well. Yet, even in this darkness, we still believe in love. But now our love is not attached to high emotion or a sense of holiness. Now God's voice is heard at yet a deeper place. The spring returns with more than we thought was lost, and our sorrow turns to joy.

The radical love we have for God is not preceded by drum rolls or trumpets. There does not have to be lightning and thunder and our hearts don't have to burst. Sometimes radical just means "deeply rooted." Our love for God, deeply rooted in the essence of life, may show itself quietly, tenderly, and humbly. Perhaps others may not even notice it because of its ordinariness. Our radical love for God may manifest as unremarkably as a sigh of awe when we look up at a star-filled sky. It may be as brief as closing our eyes for just a moment as we stand in line at the grocery store, remembering God.

Radical love is not contingent on our *feeling* God's presence, but on our *believing* in the immanence of God. In the times when we do not feel the presence of God, in the times when it appears that we are all alone, our faith carries us through the unknowing. We believe in love even when love seems lost forever. For this we were born: to remain with God each day in love and devotion, and to commune with God even in the darkness.

Grounded in Real Life

We walk with God in the evening breeze. We keep vigil with God through the dark and silent night. We rise with God as the morning comes, and we work with God throughout the day. We are more than creatures of God. In the transforming light of radical love, we have become God's friends. We have not chosen God; it is God who has chosen to be intimate, familiar, and trusting with us. God has chosen us to bear the fruit of heaven.

All of our efforts to know and understand God come to nothing, but through love we discover a union more intimate than any cognition. And as we expand our belief in God as transcendent and embrace God as immanent, we no longer distinguish between the natural and the supernatural, but embrace the two as one.

The radical love we share with God becomes grounded in the reality of life. It is not a honeymoon that takes us away from our ordinary living or lifts us into rapture so sublime that we forget the wounded world of which we are a part. Our radical love for God is not an anesthetic. It is not a pleasant dream from which we refuse to awaken. Our radical love for God is *real*. It is intimate. It is life itself. It is eternal.

Now is the time for surrendering our unhallowed life and yielding to the sanctity that comes. Of ourselves we can do nothing—but connected to God, the force of love flows through us. Detached, we wither and harden, becoming useless to ourselves, to God, and to the world. The glory of life is manifested through those who choose to remain connected, dependent, and receptive to the radical love of God.

God loves us through ourselves and through one another. In God's love we laugh and cry, and live from day to day. We choose to walk the way of sacrifice. We are willing to be true to our humanity, even unto death; and we transcend the limits of our temporal selves and enter into the oneness of all.

We die to all that is not love. Our attention is on God, and we avoid anything that will distract us from this sublime focus. Touched by the radical love of God, we also love radically, and the love we share with God is known through our living.

Pure Intention

The temptation that Jesus encountered in the desert was the same temptation that we face, that is, to look upon God as a provider of our basic needs and our protector from harm. To focus exclusively on these aspects of God is to misunderstand our relationship with the divine. Our relationship with God must be founded first and foremost on our radical love for God and on our pure intention to live and die according to the will of God.

We love God, not in order to be protected or saved from enemies, but just because God is God. The question is not, "What can God give to me?" But rather, "What does God want to give to the world through me?"

When we choose radical love, we abandon all the other treasures of the heart and seek only the will of God. This is not an abandonment of self, but a giving away of self, an emptying of self that is motivated by our radical love for God and for all creation. Our personality is not lost; it is tempered and honed to better serve God. We love God by making choices in our life that are congruent with what we believe is the will of God. We love God by being conscious of and present to God every moment of the day. We talk with God and listen with our heart to what might be revealed. We love God by tending to ourselves spiritually, mentally, and physically in order that we may be better able to do God's work in the world.

For radical love, it is not enough to do the will of God. We must also *will* the will of God. For radical love, it is not enough to stop hating our enemies and those who do us harm. We must also actively love them and be concerned for their welfare. For radical love, it is not enough that we stay conscious of the present moment. We must also love consciously in that moment.

When we love God, we love all human beings, and when we love all human beings, we love God. We cannot love one without the other.

> *Whoever does not love does not*
> *know God, for God is love.*
> 1 John 4:8

CHAPTER FIVE

INSTINCT OF THE SOUL

Returning to Our Essence

God infuses our spirit with radical love even before we leave the womb, and that love accompanies our soul as we enter into death. In between, love sustains us through the days and nights of our lives. It brings into union that which belongs together, but which has been separated. It is the basic instinct within us that weds spirit to soul.

Radical love is our natural state of being, and the work of spirituality is to return us to this original state. To love God and one another is more than a commandment; it is a conscious re-emergence of our essence.

In the beginning of our love-experience with God we may cling to an ecstasy of otherworldliness, but gradually love grounds us in the reality of the wounded world in which we live. We may at first be inebriated with the idea of holiness and obsessed with our pursuit of saintliness, but love sobers us up quickly as we are thrown into the cold water of humility. Aware of the darkness within us, as well as the light, we accept ourselves totally and unconditionally. We may want to associate with the omnipotence of God, but radical love reminds us abruptly of our powerlessness. We may not want to leave the oceanic experience of prayer and contemplation, yet God bids us to arise and go among those who need the touch of love.

Radical love is powerful, but it does not put itself up against any other power. Its power comes from its inclusiveness of all that is, just as it is. Radical love does not conquer the world by force of might, but by small, unnoticed, individual gestures prompted by the heart. It does not advertise its acts of kindness or the sacrifices made on behalf of others. "So whenever you give alms, do not sound a trumpet before you, as the hypocrites do in the synagogues and in the streets, so that they may be praised by others. Truly I tell you, they have received their reward. But when you give alms, do not let your left hand know what your right hand is doing, so that your alms may be done in secret; and your Father who sees in secret will reward you" (Matt 6:2–4).

Radical love is free. It cannot be compelled or coerced in any way. It cannot be bought, and it is not owed. Radical love simply *is*. We can create favorable conditions for it to grow, such as openness, receptivity, and quiet, but ultimately, radical love comes spontaneously. It comes when we least expect it, and it comes in the ordinary times and places of our life.

Touching the Lives of Others

To live from radical love is to live from our ground of being, which is God. Such a life is pervaded with a sense of well-being, courage, and hope. It touches the lives of others in beneficial, healing ways. We say we love those whom we serve, but in reality it is God who loves and serves through us.

When we love radically with God's love, we do not love others because we find good in them, but just because they are who they are. To love others as God loves us is to value their life and their growth. We do this by responding to their needs, by respecting them, and appreciating their individual uniqueness. We encourage them to become who they want to be in an atmosphere of support and freedom.

Those whom we love may or may not deserve our love, but it doesn't matter, because our love, which is rooted in God, is unilateral and contingent on absolutely nothing. It is not that we love the unlovable; rather, because we are of God, we consider no one unlovable.

Radical love has the power to change our character, to govern our impulses, soften our enmity, and ennoble our treatment of others. But loving others does not mean that we allow them to take advantage of us or manipulate us into doing what they want us to do. Permitting that would not come from love, but from our desire to affect how others feel toward us. Our work of love is done with no interest in the opinion of others. What comes of love just comes and does not seek to impress even God. Radical love is not about the lover but about the beloved.

Radical love compels us to be honest with those whom we love, but to do so we must first be true to ourselves. Our love for others moves us to share our light with them, but we are foolish indeed if we attempt to serve others at the expense of neglecting the Source of light itself.

Much of what we call love is really ego-centered interplay between persons. It is a relationship based on duality and separation. Radical love emanates from the divine. It is inherently one, yet includes the lover, the beloved, and love itself. It is not based on our desire for union, but on the actuality of union with all that is.

Liberating Our Beloved

The radical love of God does not bind us in any way. There are no obligations, no expectations, and no requirements. Radical love is by its very nature a *liberating* force.

It should never be confused with attachment, desire, attraction, awe, infatuation, pleasure, or dependency. Love that is based on need lasts only as long as the need and thus is not really love. If our need is what initially turns us toward God, then it has already accomplished a great deal. Beyond that, a prayer of love would have us surrender to the will of God and devote our attention to God. In such a prayer we offer ourselves as servants of creation, even to the point of suffering and death.

Radical love is not enmeshment. It is not an entanglement of persons that makes them indistinguishable from one another. Radical love encourages the separate identity of the beloved. It is the freedom to be one's self that allows for the union of souls. We must first develop our ego boundaries before we can transcend them in love. Radical love leaves freedom in its wake. It can cherish the beloved, yet avoid attachment caused by neediness or fear. Love understands that life is change and that nothing lasts forever, but it dares to invest because love is never wasted.

When we love one another with the radical love of God, it transforms us from self-seeking to self-giving, from wanting to possess or control others to working for their freedom.

Radical love is not of the past or the future; it can only be given and received in the *now*. It is in this moment of consciousness that we commend our souls to God. It is in this moment of authenticity that we accept ourselves just as we are. And it is in this moment of compassion that we respond to those who suffer.

Radical love builds where hate destroys; it pacifies where aggression disturbs; and it opens where pride closes. It is through our love that life reaches its fullest potential, and it is through our love that God lives in the world.

Accepting without Discrimination

Radical love is blind. When we love radically, we love without prejudice. We love others independently of who they are and what they look like. We love them regardless of their socioeconomic background, their age, their level of education, or their loveliness. Our love is extended to the powerful as well as the helpless, the grateful as well as the ungrateful. Everything and everyone is intrinsically lovable to God.

It is one thing to talk about loving humanity; it is quite another to actually love the rude man who cuts in front of us in line or the intrusive salesperson who phones us just as we are sitting down for dinner. We can pray for the welfare of the world, but more potent is our prayer for the particular woman who just received a diagnosis of cancer and for the little girl who was raped by marauders in the refugee camps of Darfur or India. Love is universal, yet its power is in the details.

To be of any benefit to the beloved, love must be demonstrated, that is, it must be offered in deed as well as word. A little boy is told that he is loved by his father, but that means nothing to him since his busy father spends no time with him at all. We may profess our love for the poor, and yet not be willing to give even a dollar to the homeless man on the street, because we're afraid that he might misuse the money.

Radical love opens us up to the vast terrain of life with all its peaks and valleys. Radical love of life means that we accept life just as it is. From day to day it may include grief and sorrow, suffering and disappointment, as well as joy and fulfillment, but we embrace all of it, regardless of what life brings.

I will love them freely...
Hosea 14:4

CHAPTER SIX

THE FRUIT OF
THE VINE

Patience and Kindness

Patience comes of radical love. We are not patient in order to love, but rather, because we love. When we love, our beloved is the most important thing to us; therefore, we can bear provocation from others without reacting automatically. We don't become annoyed at others just because they are not meeting our expectations.

The quality of what we build and the beauty of what we create are at the mercy of our patience. That which is lasting in structure and effect is that to which we have given patience. Our patience deems us humble artisans, doing the best we can with what we possess in time, treasure, and talent.

With patience, the means become as important as the ends. Setting aside our own agenda to be for another is a loving gesture that comes of patience, as does stopping to listen attentively to a child or taking the time to just sit and be with an elderly person.

When we love radically, our focus is on God alone, so we can accept misfortune and even pain without complaining, getting angry, or sulking. We can allow events to take their course even if they take longer than we anticipated. The patience that comes from radical love quiets us and keeps us steady as we persevere through the difficult events of life. Because we live in and for God, loving patience helps us to be diligent in everything we do.

Kindness may manifest as a major sacrifice or a simple gesture. We may decide to give away half of what we possess to feed the poor or we may decide to smile at a stranger. We may dare to rescue a child from a burning house or we may dare to place a reassuring hand on the shoulder of a bereaved mother. Radical love has no barriers to its expression.

Kindness is the gift of a generous heart. In the miracle of generosity one person shares from limited means, and inspires others to do the same. The generosity that love inspires has to do with giving liberally from the heart. It does *not* mean that we share only from our surplus, but also from that which we cherish and need. But it does not mean that we give it all away either. Rather, we love ourselves in the process and share with ourselves as well as others. Acts of kindness that are not founded on self-love result in the loss of vital boundaries and often eventually end in resentment.

The spirit of generosity gives freely, that is, without expectations of compensation or the acquisition of power or credit. It is a spirit that supersedes greed and insecurity. It is the spirit of oneness. The miracle of generosity manifests itself not only in the sharing of our material goods, but in the sharing of our minds, our hearts, and our spirits with one another.

In kindness, we may be nice to someone who has just been rude to us; we may treat the store clerk with respect and dignity regardless of his mood; we may write a letter to a friend or stranger just to let her know that someone in the world is thinking of her. Kindness compels us to leave our place of comfort and reach out beyond ourselves to serve the needs of others. It is amazing how so little can do so much when it is shared.

Humility and Joy

God loves us just as we are. We do not need to wear masks; we do not need to create false images of ourselves; and we do not have to pretend to be who we are not. God calls us to humility and to honesty about ourselves. In love and humility we honor our weaknesses as well as our strengths, and we recognize our limitations as well as our potentialities. In love and humility we acknowledge our liabilities as well as our assets, and we let go of our inordinate ambition to be more than we are. In love and humility we make the best of the conditions in which we find ourselves, and we develop all that has been given to us and use it to the best of our abilities.

If we are dependent on the radical love of God for everything, if we are but the branch on the vine, if we are merely the reflection of God in the world, what is it that we can boast about? It is one thing to honor and respect the being that God has created us to be, and it is quite another to take credit for it and brag about it! The pride of self-sufficiency and the delusion of independence strip us of faith and sink us into the deep waters of desperation. Moonlight is not sunlight, but merely its reflection. We are not God, but merely created in the image of God. To arrogate to ourselves superiority to others in any way is to pretend what is not true. Radical love is by nature humble, and humility is truth. Pretentiousness is not truth, but a lie that we live by when we do not love ourselves.

Wrongdoing comes about as a result of not facing up to the truth. When we fail to base our life on the reality before us we are operating on false premises, and this leads to mistakes and wrongful actions. It is only when radical love compels us to stay in the present and confront what is, that we can respond with right action. When we are God-conscious, that is, when we are living in truth, we know which actions come from love and which ones come from a lack of love. We know and care about which actions hurt others and which work for their benefit.

To rejoice in truth means that we live according to the radical love of God, even if it requires sacrifice on our part. We live in joy. But joy is not a goal for us or a reward for living well. It is simply the consequence of aligning our minds, hearts, and bodies with divine love. When our souls are in congruence with love, then we are filled with joy.

Joy is the hidden treasure that we discover in the most unlikely places. It is found in the common ordinary fabric of life. If we wait for joy only on the mountaintop while we remain oblivious to it in the valley, we will never know it. The joy that comes in the morning comes not in spite of the night but because of it. This is the paradox of joy. It is not to be found separate and apart from the pain of life but integrated with it as we live out our humanity. Joy is the rose that blooms among the thorns: "[Y]ou will have pain, but your pain will turn into joy" (John 16:20).

Joy comes to us when our sense of beauty is touched by a hummingbird as it flits among spring flowers. It comes to us when our sense of humor is tickled by the antics of a child. It comes to us when intimacy is awakened in us by the physical or emotional touch of our beloved. Joy comes to us when we stop seeking happiness through pleasure and possessions and seek only the realm of God within.

Tolerance and Forgiveness

Radical love opens our mind to possibilities. It moves us to honor and respect others, even when they are different from us or think differently than we do. In radical love, we do not insist on being right all the time, but instead, we listen with open minds to what others believe to be true.

The tolerance that comes with radical love opens up many worlds to us. We are not limited to a prejudiced view of people. We tolerate differences in cultures, religions, and ways of living. Respecting and honoring differences provides us with a many-splendored view of life.

Radical love allows us to be less than perfect. When we don't have to be perfect, we also don't have to do everything perfectly or demand that others meet our standards for perfection. When things have to be "just so" for us, then we are insisting on our own way and discounting the way of others. Radical love allows for "good enough." It helps us to take life as it comes, so that we aren't always battling it and trying to shape it to our ideal.

In radical love our beloved takes the forefront and we fade into the background. It's not that we stop mattering to ourselves or that we neglect our own needs. Rather, we spend our mental, emotional, and spiritual energy loving the other, and thus we have no energy left to whine or complain about what we would prefer. Rather than be irritated because things don't go our way, we focus on what we are going to do with what is. Rather than resent others for not meeting our expectations or for hurting us, we love them, and with love comes forgiveness.

When we are angry or resentful toward another it saps us of our life energy. It is like being possessed by an alien force that we cannot control. Radical love enables us to take a different course. We can decide on the spot not to hold against the other person what they have done to hurt us. It is a cognitive decision that frees our whole being from the shackles of bitterness and hate, resentment and anger. It is a letting go of that which is toxic to us, and consequently to the whole world.

As we decide not to hold against someone what they have done to us, we re-empower ourselves to respond to them with loving-kindness. This does not mean that we don't hold them accountable for what they did. It does not mean that we just ignore that which hurt us. It means that as we deal with the offender, we do it with compassion and we do it in the light of love.

We have all witnessed cruel and heinous acts perpetrated on the innocent; surely there must be a limit to what can be forgiven. Yet, it is when our hearts are darkest that the light of forgiveness is needed most. Radical love empowers us to forgive the unforgivable. Radical love breaks the cycle of retribution and frees us to be different from our perpetrators.

I am the vine, you are the branches. Those who abide in me and I in them bear much fruit, because apart from me you can do nothing.
John 15:5

CHAPTER SEVEN

THE WAY OF THE SOUL

Purpose and Meaning

Life is sometimes hard to bear, but radical love makes it bearable. We assume that living with pain and suffering, disease and death is what is so hard for us to bear, and certainly this is true. What is even more unbearable for us, however, is living a loveless life. Love gives purpose and meaning even to our greatest travail, and with purpose and meaning we can bear almost anything.

Radical love is the purpose and meaning for living, but when we become disconnected from love we forget the "why" of our life and become distracted, disoriented, and desperate. We have no control over many of the events in our lives, but as human beings we are capable of determining the effect events have on us by how we perceive them. We can decide what to make out of what life gives us; we can decide what to learn from it, and we can decide how to grow from it.

Making life bearable requires intentional living and conscious loving. It is up to us to transform what is unbearable into something constructive for ourselves and others. The force of radical love within each one of us emanates from our soul. It energizes and motivates us to discover a personal and unique reason for living, a potent intentionality that gives purpose to our being and meaning to our existence.

Faith and Hope

Because radical love restores us to our original innocence, we behold the world without suspicion or cynicism. This does not mean that we are naive about the deception in the world or vulnerable to predators. It means that we believe in the power of love more than in the power of evil. It means that we believe in the goodness of persons in spite of some of their actions, and we believe in the possibility of redemption even for the worst of us.

Belief is a vibrant, provocative, and even revolutionary state of being that is born of a loving communion with God.

As a consequence of radical love we believe in something beyond ourselves, something more expansive than our limited view of reality, something that is not manifested to us except through the eye of the soul. Belief does not solve problems or do away with life's hardness, but it helps us persevere in the face of all adversity. Radical love engenders belief, and belief gives rise to hope.

We usually define hope as the feeling that what is wanted can be had or that events will turn out well. But the hope that comes from radical love is so much more than a feeling of optimism or a positive attitude toward what is to come. It is much more than wishing for or expecting something we want. It is more than clinging to a dream. The hope that comes of radical love is based on the reality of God. Our hope is in God alone.

When we come to the edge of our limitations, when we run out of runway, when of ourselves we can expect nothing, that is when we dare to hope. In our inadequacy, we hope in the supreme adequacy of God; in our littleness, we hope in the incomprehensible magnitude of God; and in our hopelessness, we cling to the holy hope of God.

There is a difference between the hope we have based on our expectations and our holy hope. Expectations impose our will onto life; holy hope opens us up to the movement of God. We hope, not for what we would prefer, but for the will of God to be done.

Endurance and Infinity

Jesus asked his followers not to work for the food that perishes, but for the food that endures for eternal life. He admonished them not to store up treasures for themselves that could be consumed by moth and rust or stolen by thieves. He told them instead to store up treasures in heaven where they would be beyond the reach of corrosion or theft. The food that is imperishable is love. The treasure that is eternal is love. Love is the manna from heaven, the treasure of our heart.

God's enduring love gave birth to us, and its abidingness will survive our death. By holy grace we were endowed with the gifts of courage, wisdom, and strength. Yet even if we were to lose these, we will never lose love. By our ambition we have gained power, possessions, and prestige. Yet even if we were to lose these, we will never lose love. Through all our trials and tribulations, through all the pain and loss of life, we cling to the only thing that matters—God's enduring love.

Loss is part of living. Nothing but God himself is forever. Relationships, possessions, circumstances—they can all end from one moment to the next. What then can we count on? What is permanent in life? If all is in transition, if life itself is change, then what will be the landmark that will guide us in our life? What will be the anchor that will hold us steadfast?

In faith we release our hold on that which will not last. We cleave instead to the constancy of love. God is a dynamic and everlasting being who calls us toward growth, unfoldment, and evolution, and yet assures us, "For I the Lord do not change" (Mal 3:6).

God has no beginning and no ending, and since God is love, love has no beginning and no ending. Love transcends the limits of time and the boundaries of life. Though everything changes and our life is in flux, love is a constant on which we rely. Even the loss of life does not mean the loss of love; for love is stronger than separation and longer than the permanence of death.

Many waters cannot quench love,
neither can floods drown it.
Song of Solomon 8:7

CHAPTER EIGHT

SALT OF THE EARTH

Poverty

Above all, Jesus was aware of his utter dependence on God. "I tell you, the Son can do nothing on his own, but only what he sees the Father doing; for whatever the Father does, the Son does likewise....I can do nothing on my own" (John 5:19, 30).

"Poverty of spirit" is not an option; it is our reality. It is not a virtue for which to strive; it is our nature. It has to do with our attitude toward what we have or don't have. To be poor in spirit is not a matter of suppressing our personality, and it has nothing to do with asceticism. It has to do with remaining true to our humanity, because to be human is to be poor, and, in the final analysis, we are all beggars.

"Blessed are the poor in spirit, for theirs is the kingdom of heaven" (Matt 5:3). As we accept our poverty, we release our illusions of security, power, wealth, or any other ephemeral treasure to which we cling. After all, the only real security we have is that which we receive from the love of God. The radical love of God does not guarantee security from harm, but security of the soul. The only real power is that which emanates from God; everything else is relatively impotent. The only real wealth is that which we can store in our heart; all else is superfluous. In our poverty of spirit we know that we are nothing in the presence of God, yet we are all. The divine paradox is that when we let go of everything we have everything.

In our poverty of spirit we lack everything except an intense longing to be with God. In our emptiness, we become a receptacle for the radical love of God. In our woundedness, we are bonded in compassion with a suffering world. In our incompleteness, we keep turning back to God. In our weakness we find our strength, and in our brokenness we seek a wholeness that transcends the self.

The other side of love is poverty. It is love that has impoverished us, and it is love that transforms our poverty into an abundant life in God. When we love with the radical love of God, we no longer stand alone as self, but we become one with our beloved in the realm of heaven.

Grief

Inherent in love are loss and mourning. Radical love enables us to face the reality of our losses and to experience all that comes for us emotionally, physically, and spiritually. We die a little with each loss, and then we are resurrected into a new life of eternal gratitude, deep appreciation, and radical love.

When Jesus was told that Herod had beheaded his cousin John, "he withdrew from there in a boat to a deserted place by himself" (Matt 14:13). He needed time to be alone and mourn. On another occasion, when he saw his friend Mary crying for her dead brother, Lazarus, "he was greatly disturbed in spirit and deeply moved....Jesus began to weep. So the Jews said, 'See how he loved him'" (John 11:33, 35). Jesus understood the wound of loss and the healing way of grief.

"Blessed are those who mourn, for they will be comforted" (Matt 5:4). Grief shakes us to our foundation, and we are moved to a deeper part of our being. Our grief forces us to a depth of feeling that is below anything that we have ever experienced. We descend into a sorrow so deep that it seems joy is lost to us forever. In the midst of our grief it is very hard to pray. We become spiritually dry, and it seems our faith is also lost. We feel abandoned by God in the midst of our travail.

To love wholeheartedly that which is impermanent is to celebrate the ephemeral. Birth and death are the boundaries of the body, but love has no perimeter. Radical love is stronger than death. Though the ones whom we love may die, their essence lives on in us. Though we may miss their physical presence, a more subtle connection continues, and a more complete relationship is formed. Physical life ends, but love is eternal.

Through the loss and grief we are made stronger. We become more compassionate to the pain of others, and we gain a new insight into life and death. Even in the face of death, we are called to experience our life to the fullest and to respond to it with passion. We are changed dramatically by our grief. We will eventually be all right, but we will never be the same.

Eventually, we realize that God has been with us all the while, sharing in our loss, our pain, and our tears. God has been there all along, giving us the strength and courage to make it through the long, dark night. Through our loss and grief we come to realize that our old self has died and a new person has been born. We realize too that only God, who mourns with us, can lead us back to love; and only God, who dies with us, can lead us back to life.

Meekness

In meekness we release our hold on our illusion of control. In meekness we are completely honest with ourselves about ourselves, yet our self-love never wavers. To be meek is to be humble, that is, to acknowledge and live according to our assets and liabilities, our strengths and weaknesses, and our potentialities and limitations. In meekness we stay grounded and simple in our living, and we appreciate all that we have inherited as children of God.

In humility, we let go of our inordinate ambition to be more than we are, and we develop all that has been given to us. We are the word God speaks, and we are expressed in congruence with our reality, grounded in our basic nature, and true to our inheritance.

Jesus was not worldly, but he was *earthy*, down to earth, human, and approachable. He was not an aggressive conqueror of people, but a nurturing and inspiring voice that spoke to the hearts of people, inviting them to follow.

"Blessed are the meek, for they will inherit the earth" (Matt 5:5). In our meekness we accept the reality of life just as it is. We become meek by declaring ourselves open, available, and receptive to God. We take on a different perspective about ourselves; we enter into self-forgetfulness, and go beyond ourselves to God and to all creation. It is through our basic humanity that our intrinsic divinity is revealed.

In our meekness we realize that by ourselves we can do nothing. We move by the power of God. When we come to know this, we allow God to live and love through us. But it takes courage to be meek because then we are vulnerable before the world.

Meekness brings gentleness into our lives, especially in the way we treat ourselves and others. Meekness has to do, not so much with softness, as with consideration, thoughtfulness, and being non-judgmental. In meekness we are willing to provide a place for others in our circle of radical love.

Hunger and Thirst

We hunger and thirst for heavenly ways. More than anything else in life we want to do the will of God. Nothing short of communion with God will fill us; and only the nectar of love will quench our thirst. This yearning propels us through life. It is our reason to live.

We have a natural appetite for God, yet how easily we go hungering and thirsting for that which cannot fulfill us. How often we pursue the treasures of our lesser selves. How sad when our desire for the things that do not last dulls our appetite for that which is eternal. Yet Jesus reminds us, "Blessed are those who hunger and thirst for righteousness, for they will be filled" (Matt 5:6).

Jesus hungered and thirsted for communion with God. Like any other human being, he needed food and water to survive physically, but for the survival of his soul, he was utterly dependent on what he received from God. This was the same life-giving water and manna that he offered to others.

The righteousness that we embrace goes beyond goodness and morality. We acknowledge the nature of God within us and experience the divine energy flowing through us.

You are the salt of the earth.
Matthew 5:13

CHAPTER NINE

LIGHT OF THE WORLD

Mercy

We respond to life with mercy. As we allow for our imperfect world, we allow for our own imperfection, for we are of this world. As we release from bondage those who are indebted to us, we also release ourselves. As we forgive ourselves, we are freed to go and live a better day.

Radical love is not contingent on forgiveness; rather, it's the other way around. It takes radical love to break through the walls of hurt, anger, and vengeance so that forgiveness may come. Without radical love to motivate forgiveness, it becomes just an inauthentic gesture.

Jesus was often moved by love and compassion for those who were lost. He forgave those who had strayed, and he treated them with loving-kindness. He believed in passing on the mercy of God to others. "Be merciful, just as your Father is merciful" (Luke 6:36). In response to the legalistic religiosity that surrounded him, including burnt offerings and sacrificial rituals, he said, "Go and learn what this means, 'I desire mercy, not sacrifice'" (Matt 9:13).

"Blessed are the merciful, for they will receive mercy" (Matt 5:7). Like the dawning of a new day, mercy grants a second chance in life. No matter what we have done or failed to do, in the wake of our repentance comes our absolution. We are forgiven and made whole again. God looks beyond our misdeeds to the state of our being, and believes in us even when we have stopped believing in ourselves. We are changed by the mercy that is shown to us. Our self-righteousness turns to generosity; our indignation turns to compassion; and our sense of justice turns to mercy.

Radical love moves us to forgive even the worst offenders. The healing power of radical love is evident when perpetrators of evil are forgiven by their victims. Such forgiveness does not deny the reality of the harm done; the offending act is clearly seen as bad. But love does not see the offending person as inherently bad. Radical love prompts radical forgiveness.

As we are forgiven by God and by those whom we have hurt, we are moved to forgive those who have trespassed against us. We restore the soul of those whom we forgive; we give new life where all seems lost; we heal the affliction that comes with guilt; and we pass on no less than we receive from the loving grace of God. We do not know where the circle of mercy begins or ends; we know only that it is the circle of God's radical love.

Purity of Heart

We respond to life with purity of heart. Inherent in our humanity is a deep yearning to be with God, and to be enveloped and sustained by God's unconditional, radical love. To seek God with our whole being is the instinct of our soul. For this we were born: to remain with God each day in love and devotion, and to commune with God through the darkness and the unknowing. The heart is our core, our inner self, the seat of our mind and will. It is our source of life; here we are at one with God.

"Blessed are the pure in heart, for they will see God" (Matt 5:8). To love God above all and to live accordingly is our purpose in life. All else comes of this. To respond to life with single-heartedness is to live for the one thing necessary and to leave all else behind. From the radical love we have for God, comes our ability to love ourselves and others.

We are called to be awake and alert to the life around us, and to be conscious of our own reality. We set aside illusions of what we would prefer to be. Above all, we are called to surrender totally and completely to the God of our heart. Here is where our treasure is. Our heart belongs to God.

The life of Jesus was single-heartedly devoted to God. He believed that our primal response to life was to love God with our whole being. When we love with the love of God, we no longer stand alone as self, but become one with our beloved. As a result of this wholehearted love of God, Jesus saw God in everything and everyone. He saw God in the valley of despair and the peak of ecstasy, in the profane and the sacred, in the believer and the nonbeliever. There was no place, instance, or person in which Jesus did not experience God.

In prayer and contemplation we rest in loving attention to God. We are conscious that God lives in us and loves through us. God is with us every moment of our life; purity of heart is our attentiveness to that presence.

Peace

We respond to life with peace. It is not peace at any cost or peace that shies away from necessary confrontation; neither is it peace that guarantees calm and tranquility. Rather, it is peace of soul that lets us be still even in the midst of the storm, peace that offers reconciliation of polarities, integration of our scattered parts, and love of our enemies.

When we respond to life with peace, we come from strength, not weakness; courage, not cowardice. The peace with which we respond remembers that no matter who we are or how separated we have become, we are all parts of the whole; we are one.

Jesus said to his disciples, "Peace I leave with you; my peace I give to you." But then he added, "I do not give to you as the world gives." The peace that Jesus offered was not that of accord or passivity. It had more to do with the faith and the courage to overcome fear and anxiety. "Do not let your hearts be troubled, and do not let them be afraid" (John 14:27). The peace of Jesus was not the peace that comes at the cost of our soul. It was the peace that comes even through hardship and conflict, disharmony and rejection.

"Blessed are the peacemakers, for they will be called children of God" (Matt 5:9). Peace is not contingent on the ease with which we live, and it has little to do with peaceful circumstances. In fact, peace can be ours in the midst of trouble. Peace has to do with how we respond to the moment before us. It does not come with the removal of external problems but with the internal awareness that we are not alone as we face them. In God-consciousness we can cope with whatever comes our way. Peace overcomes us amid chaos and indecision when we realize that we live in God.

The way of peace is not always the path of least resistance. "Do not think that I have come to bring peace to the earth; I have not come to bring peace, but a sword" (Matt 10:34). The peace of Jesus was the peace that comes with conviction and the willingness to give up everything for the sake of God.

The healing peace of God is ours even in the midst of the tempest. We need not wait for the turmoil in our life to subside. Peace comes when we open to the integrating love of God, even in the most disintegrating circumstances, and when we allow ourselves to rest in God's union, even as we are pulled in many directions. Internal peace sometimes means that we must be willing to live without external peace. Peace is the consequence of letting go in faith and waiting for God in trusting surrender. Peace comes when we love God more than peace itself.

Courage

We respond to life with the courage of conviction. To seek after righteousness is to seek harmony with God. But our fidelity to God sometimes places us at odds with the world around us. To be persecuted is not, in and of itself, a virtue to be pursued; it is merely the consequence of living out the radical love of God in our life. "In the world you face persecution," said Jesus. "But take courage; I have conquered the world" (John 16:33).

Courage is that energy that is grounded in the belief that we have been given all that we need to handle whatever we confront. Courage is powerful because it is rooted in love, and radical love is stronger than fear. "There is no fear in love, but perfect love casts out fear" (1 John 4:18).

The courage that enabled Jesus to conquer the world was not the bravery of the man, but the power of the heart to love unabatedly and without condition; and to live uninhibitedly and without shame. The courage was the radical love of God moving through the heart of Jesus.

"Blessed are those who are persecuted for righteousness' sake, for theirs is the kingdom of heaven" (Matt 5:10). We live by what we believe regardless of the consequences. Sometimes this means persecution from those who do not understand or from those who are threatened by what we do or who we are. With courage we stand up for what and in whom we believe, and we are willing to appear weak and to suffer for the sake of love. We overcome persecution, trouble, and tribulation by staying conscious that we are one with God.

You are the light of the world.
Matthew 5:14

CHAPTER TEN

SENT INTO THE WORLD

Becoming Disciples

What happened to the disciples of Jesus soon after his crucifixion cannot be adequately explained. These men abandoned Jesus in his greatest need, they had denied him, doubted him, and had even given up hope on him. But then, these lambs-turned-lions found their courage and followed Jesus even after his death. They remembered the words with which he had charged them: "As you go, proclaim the good news, 'The kingdom of heaven has come near.' Cure the sick, raise the dead, cleanse the lepers, cast out demons" (Matt 10:7–8). The words of Jesus apply to us as well.

Proclaim the good news. We are to tell the people that God is as close to them as their own hearts, and we are to help them understand that the radical love of God is the radical love they share with one another.

Cure the sick. We have the power to bring others to wholeness through radical love. We are to reach out not only to those who are physically ill, but to those who are emotionally and spiritually broken.

Raise the dead. We are to call to life those who are dead to the glory of their humanity, and spark in them a motivation to live fully and purposefully. We are to lead them to the fountain of hope, the adventure of faith, and the resurrection of radical love.

Cleanse the lepers. We are to welcome those who have been discarded by society, take the hand of the dejected ones, and lovingly wash their feet. Then, we are to ask forgiveness for those who have scorned them.

Cast out demons. By the example of our lives, we are to teach those who are shackled to destructive ways that the power of God's radical love sets us free. God does not destroy that within us that offends, but instead sheds a loving light on the darkest of our shadows.

Changing Lives

We are sent into the world to change the lives of others. Ours is the mission of love. We are to be there for the desperate, the broken, the wounded, and the lost. Through us, God restores the afflicted, brings life to those dead in spirit, heals the malignant, and casts out the powers of darkness.

We are sent into a world that is lacking in love, and sometimes we are bruised. We invite, but never compel. We are gentle, yet wise enough to protect ourselves. We are confident in what we say and in what we do as long as we remain God-conscious. Our work is inspired by faith, and our actions are propelled by love. We are willing to do what must be done for the sake of love. Some tasks are demeaning, others arduous and mundane. We are asked to do what is required by love.

With courage we tell others out loud what we have heard in silence and reveal to them in the light what we have learned in the darkness. This is our mission: to learn the will of God and do it, regardless of the consequences. Those who receive from us receive from God. Those who embrace the messenger, embrace God.

We are the salt of the earth. It is through us that God touches the world, through us that God is known. We spread God's radical love among the people, and let them know they count.

We are the salt that preserves the earth from self-destruction, the salt that purifies the corrupt and keeps decay from overtaking hearts. We are full of grace, but what if grace leaves us? What if love disappears? What if the flavor of our salt is gone? Then we have nothing. Then what we pass on is worthless, even harmful. But we are salted with the fire of God. Our savor is God's love. We return through prayer and contemplation to the place where God restores the flavor of our salt.

We are the light of the world. We shine before those who stumble in the dark. We enlighten those who do not understand. We cannot keep the light to ourselves. It is not meant for us alone. Of what good is the light of God that shines within us if we hide it from the world? We are set on a hill for others to behold. We set our light where others can use it to find their way. Through us the hidden is revealed; the covered is brought out into the open; and the concealed is brought to light. It is not perfection that we model to the others, not even upright living. What they see is our intense, undying love for God.

Preaching Hope

The spirit of God is upon us and lives and moves and acts through us if we allow it. We are anointed to preach the Gospel to the poor. Who are the poor? Those who are lonely, unloved, and alienated from life are the poor. Those who feel abandoned, hopeless, and rejected are the poor. Whether they are economically, emotionally, or spiritually poor, we respond to them with all that God has given us.

Preaching the Gospel does not necessarily mean evangelizing with words, although it may include this. It also means living out the Gospel message of radical love before others. The message that we preach with our words and our life has to do with God's unconditional, inalienable, and radical love for us.

God sends us to heal the brokenhearted. We, who have not been spared the pain that comes with living, are given the power to heal others through compassionate action. It seems the broken can truly minister unto the broken. The healing comes not from any spiritual magic, but from the warm and gentle treatment we administer to others. Radical love is tender. We treat with tenderness those who are close to us and those whom God has placed in our life. We listen to them; we encourage them, comfort them, and accept them without judgment. Through our care and understanding, hearts mend and tears are wiped away.

We are sent to preach deliverance to the captives. First, however, we must free ourselves from the ties that bind us to our lower selves, and then we can help others to also break away. We are all captives of something. Some of us are caught in the web of addictions. Some of us are chained to a destructive way of life. Others of us are prisoners of our memories. Preaching deliverance is preaching the powerlessness of humanity and the powerfulness of God. Such deliverance comes in the wake of desperate prayer.

We are sent to offer sight to the blind. Because we too have been blind, we know the terror of the darkness. We know that the only hope for light is through unceasing prayer and contemplation. We are sent to love one another in such a radical way that the scales of fear and prejudice fall away from our eyes. Through the sharing of the radical love of God we are able to share with each other a spiritual sight that we cannot see with our physical eyes. As we carry radical love into the world, we carry the light that overcomes the darkness.

We are sent to set at liberty those who are kept down. We are the hands of God that reach out to help a brother who has been oppressed. Through our alignment with that brother we can help him stand up and be free once again. We are the mercy of God that supports a sister in such a way that she may be liberated from the restraints of her economic circumstances. We are the compassion of God that works long and hard to alleviate the inhuman conditions under which so many live and die.

Healing Wounds

It is not a matter of asking ourselves in every case, "What is the loving thing to do?" and then doing it. Rather, when we remember that we are love, our actions take care of themselves. Perhaps this is what Saint Augustine meant when he advised that we love God and do as we please.

Radical love compels us to respond to the cries of a world that is hurting, hungering, searching for life. It demands that we use the talents we have been given to nurture, feed, and guide others. Anything that comes from us is the fruit of a vine well rooted in the soil of prayer and nurtured to fruition by the love of God. As long as we remain in God, our work is inspired by faith and our actions are vivified by love.

Through us the power of love soothes the wounds of those around us, mends their broken hearts, and gives them a sense of significance and belonging. Through us the power of radical love opens the door to understanding, invites peace, and brings harmony in the midst of dissension.

Radical love may manifest in simple, but powerful ways. Giving sincere attention to a sad and lonely man can touch his soul and lighten his burden. Just knowing that someone sees him as a person and cares about his pain can make his life bearable for yet another day. Being kind to the woman who has known only cruelty and abuse can soothe her wounded heart and begin the healing of her soul.

It is not often that we are called upon to lay down our physical life for the sake of someone else, although radical love would certainly be ready to make that sacrifice. We are, however, constantly asked to lay down our self-centered, egoistic life for the sake of someone else. Even in small ways we are given opportunities to set aside our preferences, our comfort, and our agendas, for the sake of someone else. Sometimes we inconvenience ourselves for the sake of a friend or family member; sometimes we do it for a total stranger. We lay down our life for the sake of others every time we place their welfare before ours.

No one has greater love than this,
to lay down one's life for one's friends.
John 15:13

CHAPTER ELEVEN

BLESSED BELOVED

The Way of the Cross

On the way of the cross we become aware of our impotence. If in the past we have attempted to protect ourselves with power, now we are asked to let go of all our defenses and acknowledge that the only real power comes from the radical love of God.

"If any want to become my followers, let them deny themselves and take up their cross and follow me" (Matt 16:24). To take up the cross means that we are willing to embrace suffering and allow it to transform us. On the way of the cross, we are willing to enter into our crisis wholeheartedly and God-consciously. The cross experience is the consequence of radical love. It includes faithful suffering, selfless sacrifice, purposeful living, and meaningful dying.

The way of the cross is paved with the reality of our humanity, including our vulnerability and dependency, our fragility and finitude. Here, in our poverty, we release our hold on things ephemeral and embrace that which is eternal.

The way of the cross takes us into the place of darkness, the abyss of despair, here to be at one with the forsaken, the miserable, and the crucified. We come here to bring light and compassion to our blessed beloved in the name of God.

As we open to love, we open to the suffering that comes with love. When someone we love is suffering, we suffer as well. What can bring us more agony than to know a loved one is greatly suffering? When they hurt physically, emotionally, or spiritually, it is torture to our heart. We want desperately to take their place.

The cross is the symbol of our wounded world. When we look upon the cross we see the face of the old woman in a nursing home, forgotten by her family, just waiting to die. We see the little girl who has been passed from one set of foster parents to another without a home to call her own. We see the soldier, paralyzed by weapons of war, no longer able to play with his child or take a stroll with his wife. We see the family with swollen stomachs and sunken eyes, dying slowly of starvation. We see disease, poverty, conflict, and apathy spreading in our world with impunity.

The cross of suffering is also the cross of radical love. While it alerts us to the grief, pain, and distress in the world, it also moves us to respond with self-forgetting courage, presence, and compassionate action.

Divine Energy

We fall radically in love with God and rest in the divine presence. The sense of union is ecstatic, and the devotion to our Beloved is total and consistent. Then we are asked to leave the sacred summit and descend into the abyss of a loveless world, with the mission to redeem it one person at a time. We must leave behind the language of heaven, for it will not be understood, and the mystical experience can never be explained. We return to be among the people, armed with nothing but a soul full of love.

Awakening to radical love is like having an infusion of divine energy. Our passionate longing for love is transformed into a peaceful waiting for an opportunity to love in the name of God. It is not about stirring inebriating, romantic feelings, but about releasing the potent force of eros that flows through our veins, evoking a grounded, yet vigorous response to the will of God. The marriage of eros and agape gives birth to a life of benevolent vitality and compassionate service.

When we speak of our Beloved we are not referring exclusively to God, but also to every soul that emanates from God. The language of God is love. Through prayer and contemplation our souls listen to God, and through compassionate action, our spirits pass on God's love to others. We are the love that communes with the divine, and we are the love that reaches out to touch a wounded world.

When we love, we are focused on the welfare of the ones whom we love. We nurture them and seek their physical, emotional, and spiritual well-being. We encourage their growth and we help them move toward their own fulfillment. We are not motivated to act on their behalf by the need to be needed; rather, our actions are the consequence of loving radically. Nothing is expected except for congruence between who we are and what we do.

Radical love is the divine energy that awakens our concern for the welfare of others, and moves us to act on their behalf, even at great sacrifice to ourselves. We love God by taking good care of God's creation, including our fellow human beings and the planet on which we live. We love God by accepting the life we've been given and living it to the best of our ability. We love God by allowing ourselves to become conduits for God's radical love in the world.

The Vessel of God

Blessed are we, for we are the vessel of God. It is through us that the Incarnation continues to take place. We who deem ourselves unworthy are loved greatly by God, and God has chosen to come into the world through us. "Look, the virgin shall conceive and bear a son, and they shall name him Emmanuel, which means, 'God is with us'" (Matt 1:23). We have received the seed of God. What a glorious state to find ourselves pregnant with God, and what a tremendous responsibility! How awesome to know that God is planted within us, and is being nurtured by our love. In this most intimate union we are both separate and together—two beings, one soul.

As we ponder the mystery of this sacred conception, we experience myriad emotions. We feel inadequate to bring this gift of love to full term, yet we are hopeful because it depends, not on us, but on a power beyond us. We feel excited about the life that grows within, and at the same time, we are afraid of what will be asked of us. We feel the discomfort and the burden of being stretched and distorted within as we change to accommodate our holy guest, yet we also feel the exalted joy of co-creation, and the fervent anticipation of new life.

We do not understand all that is happening to us, and we do not see the bigger picture of which we are a part, but we move ahead through our trepidation with the courage of love's abandon and faith in the perpetuity of God.

We are the basket that holds the gift of heaven. Through our life God loves the world.

Blessed Are We

Blessed are we who depend so completely on the love of God to see us through the day. We are open, available, and receptive to the grace that God bestows. We have set aside the illusion of our self-sufficiency and have embraced the reality of our poverty. With our surrender of life comes the prevalence of God.

Blessed are we who allow the pain of our loss to consume us. We will be given the courage to enter the dark night of separation, and we will find the strength to endure until the dawn.

Blessed are we who admit the truth about ourselves. In our honesty, we recognize our potential and our limitations. In our humility, we accept ourselves as we are. Our decision to drop away the masks we wear brings us the freedom to be real. When we are open to the world, the world opens to us.

Blessed are we who yearn for God. We seek sustenance for our soul, and we thirst for the nectar of heaven. Our desire for the will of God releases us from the snare of our other appetites. Now we are filled with radical love.

Blessed are we who forgive from our heart. We pardon the debts of others and release them from our hold. We cast loose the fetters of the world that they may be loosed in heaven.

Blessed are we who accept the mercy of God and are willing to pass it on.

Blessed are we who allow the ecstasy of life to overwhelm our heart. We discover joy even in suffering because we see the face of God in everything.

Blessed are we who find the quiet of God even in the battlefield of life. Our tranquility of soul does not depend on the external, but rather on the state of our inner self.

Blessed are we who dare to live according to the dictates of our heart, even in the face of persecution. Neither pain nor humiliation, neither bondage nor death, can sway us from our destiny with God.

Blessed is the one who comes in
the name of the Lord.
Matthew 23:39

CODA

*No one has ever seen God; if we love one another,
God lives in us, and his love is perfected in us.*
1 John 4:12

green press INITIATIVE

Paulist Press is committed to preserving ancient forests and natural resources. We elected to print this title on 30% post consumer recycled paper, processed chlorine free. As a result, for this printing, we have saved:

2 Trees (40' tall and 6-8" diameter)
1,057 Gallons of Wastewater
1 million BTU's of Total Energy
64 Pounds of Solid Waste
220 Pounds of Greenhouse Gases

Paulist Press made this paper choice because our printer, Thomson-Shore, Inc., is a member of Green Press Initiative, a nonprofit program dedicated to supporting authors, publishers, and suppliers in their efforts to reduce their use of fiber obtained from endangered forests.

For more information, visit www.greenpressinitiative.org

Environmental impact estimates were made using the Environmental Defense Paper Calculator. For more information visit: www.papercalculator.org.